HENRI CIRIANI

CONTEMPORARY
WORLD
ARCHITECTS

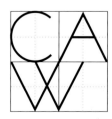

HENRI CIRIANI

Foreword by
Richard Meier

Introduction by
François Chaslin

Concept and Design by
Lucas H. Guerra
Oscar Riera Ojeda

ROCKPORT PUBLISHERS
ROCKPORT, MASSACHUSETTS

First published in the United States of America by:
Rockport Publishers, Inc.
146 Granite Street
Rockport, Massachusetts 01966
Telephone: (508) 546-9590
Fax: (508) 546-7141

ISBN 1-56496-234-2

10 9 8 7 6 5 4 3 2 1

Cover Photograph: World War 1 Museum, Péronne, France. Photograph by Jean Marie Monthiers.
Photographs on page 1, 2, and 3: Archaeological Museum. Photograph by Jean Marie Monthiers.

Printed in Hong Kong

Graphic Design: Lucas H. Guerra / Oscar Riera Ojeda
Connexus Visual Communications / Boston
Layout: Oscar Riera Ojeda
Composition: Matt Kanaracus / Codesign / Boston

CONTENTS

Foreword by Richard Meier   6
Introduction by François Chaslin   8

Works
Hospital Kitchen   14
Municipal Child Care Center   22
World War 1 Museum   34
Archaeological Museum   46
Marne Social Housing   60
Saint-Denis Social Housing and Facility   66
Evry Social Housing   74
Lognes Social Housing and Facility   82
Charcot Social Housing and Shops   90
Bercy Social Housing and Shops   98
Colombes Social Housing Facility and Shops   106
The Hague Apartment Building   112

In Progress
Groningen Towers   120
Nijmegen Towers   124

Appendix
List of Works and Credits   128
Acknowledgements   132

Foreword

BY RICHARD MEIER

In 1978 I was invited to Paris by the President of Renault, Mr. Bernard Hanon, to begin work on the design of the company's headquarters on a site adjacent to their existing Boulogne-Billancourt building. It was during this period that François Barre, then Director of Cultural Affairs at Renault, introduced me to architects in Paris whose work was most provocative. With Barre and a group of Parisian architects, I visited a great many recently completed works that, at the time, impressed me with their inventiveness, their concern for detail, and their intellectual rigor expressed in a variety of attitudes. This was a memorable moment for architecture: It was the beginning of an era in France that allowed architects and architecture to speak out; it was a time during which even very young architects in France had the opportunity to do creative research on a scale, up to then, reserved for the established.

Among the "young" architects I had the pleasure of getting to know well was Henri Ciriani. He was young, he is young, and his projects are forever young. His work was primarily in the public sector as he is an expert at public housing and loves housing.

However, as one of the most influential forces in the current French scene, he has recently extended his practice into the field of museums.

In all of his architecture there is evidence of a very serious man whose experimentation acts on many levels. His concerns with form and geometry are related to the functional organization of the program, and his expression of circulation adheres to Modernist tenets, which favor accessibility and fluidity. There is a centrality to much of his work. The hub of activity and architecture is expressed volumetrically and lyrically through light; light which is, of course, central to his architecture. The curious colors that invade his spaces personalize his work to an even greater degree than would otherwise be the case. The organization of his palette comes from the earth and the sky, and, to some extent, his iconographic reading of the space. The work in this book is an indication of his thoughts and concerns up until now. How we look forward to the expression of his future meditations on architecture.

The white concrete-faced planes of the
northern facade emphasize the unity
and the scale of the World War I Museum.
The light wells secure the individual
needs of the secondary functions (service
and dwellings) without introducing
out-of-scale details in the exterior.

Introduction

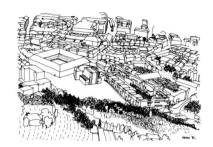

BY FRANÇOIS CHASLIN

With the 1992 opening of the World War 1 Historial in Péronne (Somme) and the completion in Spring 1995 of the Archaeology Museum in Arles (Provence), Henri Ciriani sheds the stereotype of housing and social infrastructure architect that has long plagued him in France. In so doing, he has had the opportunity to more fully demonstrate his exceptional talents for generating space and form, and for manipulating light.

The son of a Peruvian air force general, Ciriani was born in 1936. At a very young age, even before finishing his architecture degree in 1960, he built a number of private residences; and, as part of a studio in his country's Ministry of Public Works, he worked on large-scale urban design projects. Once graduated, Ciriani directed extensive housing construction (5,000 units in Ventanilla, a satellite of Lima, and several hundred units each in Matute, Mirones, Rimac, and San Felipe), an activity that lasted until 1964 when he departed for France, where he settled and took citizenship. The early projects in Peru formed Ciriani's strong-willed and progressive vision of his profession, stressing architecture's political and social implications, which he has tried to elaborate through responsive design.

In Paris, Ciriani worked in the office of architect André Gomis, while concurrently pursuing his own design by participating in international competitions (most notably the Luxembourg Airport and the Amsterdam City Hall) for which, in 1957, his strong graphics were recognized. Both distinctive and effective, Ciriani's presentation skills bestowed upon him, at a very young age, the honor of twice making the cover of *L'Architecture d'Aujourd'hui*. Throughout his career, he has remained an avid artist, devoting many hours to sketching detailed perspectives that focus on spatial quality and its composition, and even reworking competition submissions years after their refusal (such as those for the Opera at Bastille, 1983, and the National Library of France, 1989).

In 1968, Ciriani joined the Atelier d'Urbanisme et d'Architecture (Aua) at Bagnolet, a hotbed of multidisciplinary practice and social architecture during the 1960s. At its core, he was associated with the landscape architect Michel Corajoud (Borja Huidobro would join them in 1970). They formed a team that lasted until 1975, at which time he founded his own studio. Six years later, Ciriani left the Aua.

Ciriani first became involved with the Aua as illustrator of a brochure for the new town of Grenoble-Echirolles, a publication whose graphic design was a landmark. Later, with Corajoud (as self-titled "urban landscape designers"), he designed the public space for l'Arlequin, the first neighborhood in the new town. It was a ground-level passage six meters in height and one and a half kilometers long, to which public facilities were meant to graft. Influenced by contemporary advertising graphics, this strong urban gesture featured large signage and high contrast colors, and, consequently, garnered much attention.

During 1971 and 1972, the Aua architects (together with the "Taller" led by the young Catalan architect Ricardo Bofill, "a welcome breath of fresh air") joined forces for the important Evry 1 competition, which they lost to the Andrault-Parat Pyramids project. The Evry 1 competition reinforced the authority of Ciriani, but also contributed to the surfacing of tensions at the group's core (in particular, a rivalry with Paul Chemetov), which sent the studio into an irreversible decline. Their proposal for 7,000 housing units in the new town was of unequaled monumentality: a colossal, linear megastructure, 500 meters in length and twenty stories in height. Composed of articulated towers, bridge-buildings, and large oblique facades with stepped terraces, their Evry 1 submission was similar in spirit to the Italian *territoriale* experiments of the same era (for example, those of Vittorio Gregotti or Mario Fiorentino's kilometer-long apartment complex for the suburbs of Rome).

Ciriani long remained in this intellectual mode, seeking a framework that could restructure the city. He ultimately theorized his findings with the notion of the "Fil conducteur" (thread) while working on urban projects such as 7,000 housing units for Sept-Planètes at Dunkirk (1973–75) and 3,500 units for the Saint-Bonnet-le-Lac competition in the new town of l'Isle-d'Abeau (1975). In these designs, he proposed an inversion of the primary structuring element of the urban environment: "What was otherwise a void liberated by the built mass (the street) became here a solid."

Ciriani gradually evolved this principle toward the idea of strong "urban fragments" (pièces urbaines) capable of "holding" space, a theory tested in his first important built commission in France: 300 units at Noisy 2, in Marne-la-Vallee (1975–80). Noisy 2 was interpreted as a manifesto for new urban architecture that sought to renew itself with traditional typologies (as did much design of this period), but remained in continuity with the modern movement, and privileged open space instead of the street.

In an era plagued by urban sprawl and social unrest (a subject treated by sociologist Henri Lefebvre), but with a perspective committed to learning from the lessons of social planning, Ciriani promoted the fundamental importance of collective housing. He sought to prove that his "urban fragments" could foster stability and vitality in new neighborhoods. He developed dimensional facades that he described as the containing walls of public space. They were solidly supported with loggias, and characterized by a steady rhythm and calm massing that dignified social housing and communicated a reassuring image of permanence.

The same process guided his design for social housing at La Courdangle in Saint-Denis, where heavy pyramids of stepped terraces were built in a more classical context (1978–82), for the République project in Chambéry (1981–83) which was aborted by a change in municipal government, for the brilliant facade articulation at the Canal development in Evry (1981–86) and for the generous and magnificent curve of constructions in Lognes, Marne-la-Vallee (1982–86).

Ciriani remains committed to a formal approach and to collective ideals in urban design. He works toward the solid and forceful articulation of vertical and horizontal volumes. His building silhouettes, even the slabs, are enriched by a complex game of solids and voids, as in his most recent projects in the Netherlands, at Rotterdam, Groningen, Nijmegen, and The Hague.

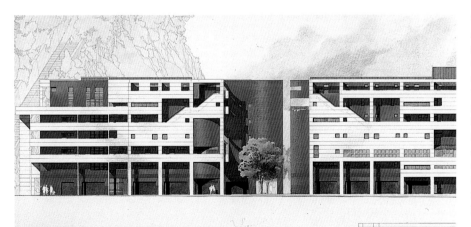

Views of Chambery Urban Fragment: Aerial view of a *campo santo*-style urban composition with Napoléon's Carre Curial, Mario Botta's theater and our dwellings as urban fragment (opposite page). Axonometric drawing showing the relation between the "wall of villas" and the transparency of the *hôtel particulier* type of units (top). Principal elevation on Avenue de la République. Ondulating vertical gap permits the horizontal urban frontage to produce the entrance to the interior residential spaces while saving a 200-year-old plane tree (left).

With regards to housing interiors, Ciriani has reached a somewhat pessimistic (or simply, realistic) conclusion. Asserting that there exists in this field a set of invariable features, he has never sought to radically modify domestic lifestyle. He has, instead, focused his efforts on working with the effects of light to shape space. Rather than flood an interior with light, Ciriani attempts to dilate volumes so that ten square meters appear as twelve. He has often succeeded in setting up exquisite compositions of light and shadow, and even, at times, of domestic monumentality. Such is the case in the duplex units of social housing on rue du Chevaleret in Paris (1987–91), which appear as small stacked villas, or those more open to the landscape, which he designed overlooking the park in Bercy (1991–94). In the Stalingrad-Marceau development at Colombes (1992–95), while densifying a suburban town center and working with a very strict set of codes for French social housing, Ciriani varied a series of typologically sophisticated units.

Concerned that each of his works is viewed as a model that contains a pedagogical lesson, he has explored several different quantities of interior architecture, of passage in continuous space, and of color. This experience is especially evident in his two museums; but it is also the case in his more modest public works such as the day care center in Saint-Denis (1978–1983), the community center in Lognes (1986–87), and the infant care facility in Torcy (1986–89).

Less interested in construction than in the combination of materials, and appreciative of reinforced concrete for its smoothness, abstraction, and perfect plasticity, Ciriani is in search of visual emotion, optical textures, colors, and forms. He has developed a kind of phenomenological intuition for architecture, pursued for what could be termed its intrinsic truth. There is, in this research, an undeniable metaphysical and spiritual dimension, especially in his tendency to venerate space and natural light. Light is sovereign in the World War 1 Historial in Péronne (1987–92). A work of rare serenity, Ciriani has brilliantly played on the theme of architectural promenade, first expressed by Le Corbusier, composing a fluid and flexible itinerary, and elegantly posing his building on the banks of a pond against the ruined fortress of Péronne.

The archaeological museum in Arles (1983–95), designed to conserve this Provencal town's vast collections of Roman artifacts, is sited on the banks of the Rhône River. Here, Ciriani selected the equilateral triangle for its plan, seeming to reference the strong geometry of Roman buildings. In fact, what he attempted was a subdivision of this basic geometry, deceptively simple in appearance but extremely difficult to manipulate and, without doubt, the least explored form in architecture. In this building, which weds concrete to large expanses of bright blue lacquered glass, he has executed a work of mature articulation and carving in plan, configuring the collections in a spiral movement around a central patio. The Museum is anchored to its site by the reach of its outstretched flanks, which appear as wings surpassing the angles of the triangle. Large windows act as magnificent frames for the riverscape, a refreshing view under the intense Mediterranean sun.

This gamble in abstraction, in any case theoretical (which otherwise he could have lost), is revealing of Ciriani's process and of an ambition that challenges him to confront formal difficulties. In fact, Ciriani wishes first and foremost to be a teacher and an explorer of the rich potential of modern space. He has painstakingly dissected its rules of organization; and, he has analyzed its aesthetic and physical effects. Ciriani is an individual who seeks order and fidelity. He is committed to modernism over novelty, to consistency and long maturation. His detractors are quick to criticize an orthodoxy that they decry as academic. Only wanting to see in his work the repetition of old tenets of the modern movement, they reproach him for staying aloof of debates and for lacking a sense of the contemporary.

Henri Ciriani (awarded the French National Prize for Architecture in 1983) enjoys, however, considerable acclaim among students. Appointed in 1969 to found the School of Architecture of Paris No. 7 (UP7), where he taught until 1977, before moving with his students to the School of Architecture of Paris No. 8 (now Belleville), this warm teacher displays extraordinary charisma. His clever vocabulary, the aphorisms by which he translates spatial

impressions, the enthusiasm that he demonstrates, and especially, the very structured program he has designed since 1978 with his colleagues from Groupe Uno, have attracted several generations of highly motivated students. In ever-increasing ranks, Ciriani's former students demonstrate a particular competence in their art, sometimes even virtuosity, and excel in competitions.

This is the only solidly constituted position in architecture that has appeared in France in recent years in answer to fertile but diffused tendencies that manifest transparency, impermanence, and a desperate search for meaning (parallels to the philosophical texts of Virilio and Baudrillard). These two currents express two irreconcilable visions of modernity in terms of the artistic and social responsibilities of the architect. The diffused current tends to accept contemporaneity in all its forms, including chaos and the destruction of traditional categories of beauty and social relevance. Fascinated by the aimless drift of the world, they feed on reality in all its forms.

Henri Ciriani remains in the more idealistic modern tradition that favors light (in all senses of the word). The tradition that sought to serve social progress with the new aesthetic (or at least symbolize that progress is possible) and believed contemporary architecture must be a cause and not a simple style. Even for those who do not, however, share this optimism, there is, in his mission to construct with light, something therapeutic and comforting. Beyond dogma, beyond the often doctrinal tone of his statements, there is something reassuring in this firm attitude that braces us against the vast panorama of mourning for dead utopias that has splintered our societies for more than twenty years.

BIBLIOGRAPHY   COLLECTIVE: Henri Ciriani, Ifa-Electa Moniteur, Paris, 1984/ H.CIRIANI: le Fil conducteur, unpublished research, Plan Construction, Paris, 1977/ H.CIRIANI (with C.Vié): L'Architecture de l'espace moderne, unpublished research, Ministère de l'Urbanisme, Paris, 1987/ P.BLIN: l'Aua, mythe et réalités, Electa-Moniteur, Paris, 1988/ J.LUCAN: France, architecture 1965–1988, Electa-Moniteur, Paris, 1989/ J.PETIT: Ciriani, architecte de lumière, Fidia edizioni d'arte, Lugano, 1996/ Revue AMC, No.14, déc.1986/ *L'Architecture d'Aujourd'hui*, No. spécial 282, sept.1992

East-west section showing the relation of the Péronne historical museum's exhibition spaces to the entrance as well as to natural light (opposite page top). The Arles archaeological museum roof landscape—with its belvedere and central stairs as triangular anchor—relates the roof garden to the patio of the exhibition spaces (top). Interior of the cafeteria's sunken space with framed vistas of the old city (left). The equilateral triangle whose sides of linear planes are reduced as they get close together, never meeting so that the initial geometry can adapt to context and function (overleaf).

Works ▶

Hospital Kitchen

66 SAINT ANTOINE HOSPITAL
PARIS, FRANCE

The brief for this competition called for a new kitchen to accommodate a staff of 30 serving 3,000 meals a day in a large metropolitan hospital. Situated in central Paris, the hospital developed by fragmented accretion, like all institutional facilities built over a 100-year period.

Located on the north side of the rue de Cîteaux, the site context is urban in-fill that poses the challenge of mediating the opposing scales of two adjacent buildings. To one side is a tall apartment building of typical Parisian street-scale; to the other side, a hospital-owned, two-story neoclassical building with a third-floor addition. The building plot is approximately 30 meters square, and all access is from the hospital grounds to the rear. Without the need for access from the street, an opportunity existed to highlight the formal issues of "facade."

The free plan exemplifies an essential tenet of Modernism: that space be unbounded and flowing. Seminal heroic schemes for the program's service aspects (storage, preparation, and cooking) anchor one corner of the kitchen plan, which liberates the rest of the space. This dichotomy provides the basis for organization, distinguishing between service spaces and serving spaces (point of distribution of the meals). The service spaces form a wall that limits two sides of the free plan to contain the square space in which the food is put on plates.

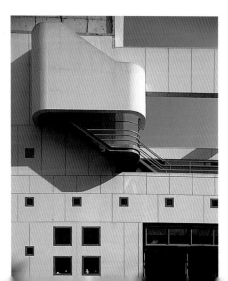

This serving space opens on the diagonal toward the hospital and the sun. Inside, the modern concept of the free plan transforms the program from a plain hospital-kitchen into something akin to a workers' club, bathed in sunlight. The composition—layered planes with their simple rectilinear openings, slip-form concrete curves, the grid of pilotis that supports the roof garden—evolved rationally from the manipulation of contemporary construction practices.

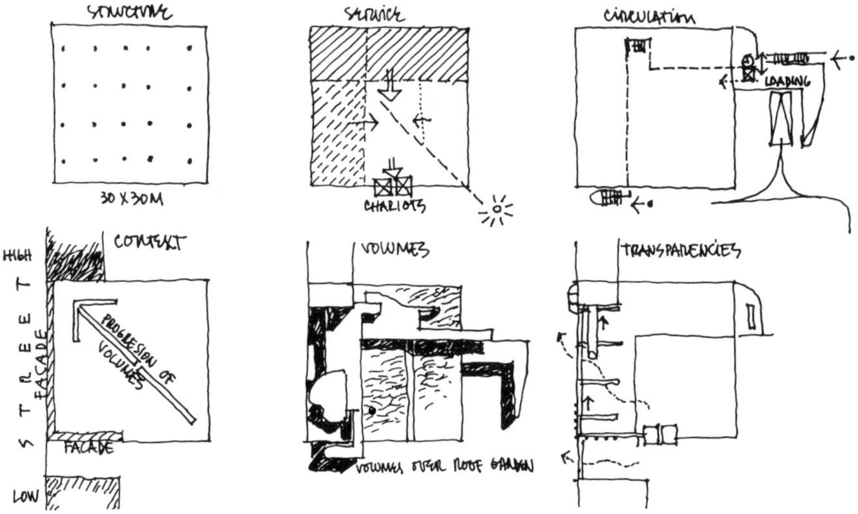

STRUCTURE

30 X 30M

SERVICE

CHARIOTS

CIRCULATION

LOADING

CONTEXT

HIGH

STREET

FACADE

PROGRESSION OF VOLUMES

FACADE

LOW

VOLUMES

VOLUMES OVER ROOF GARDEN

TRANSPARENCIES

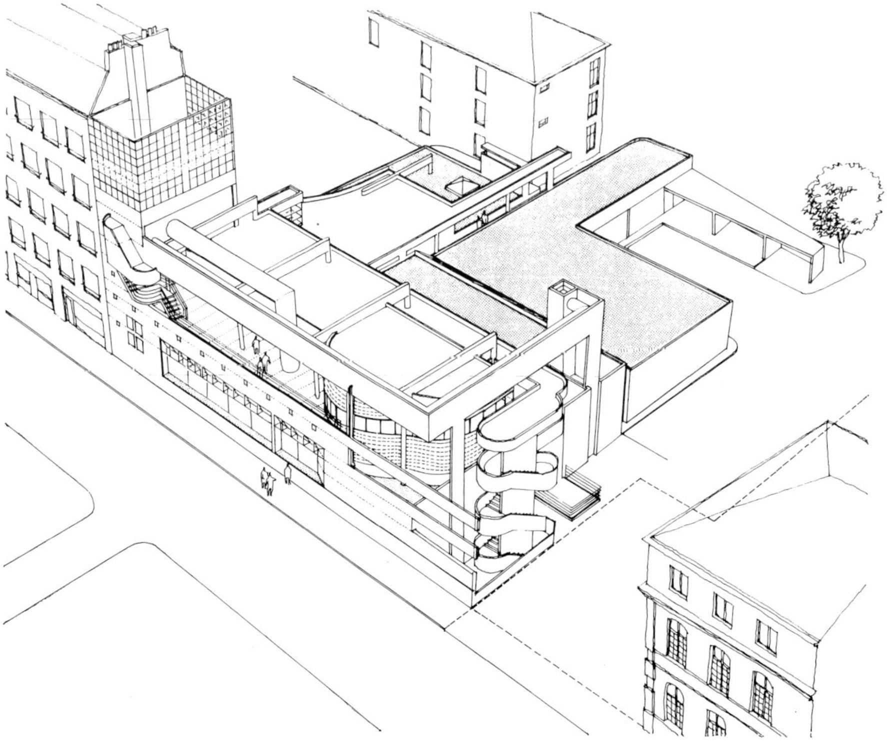

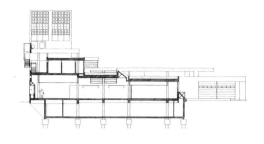

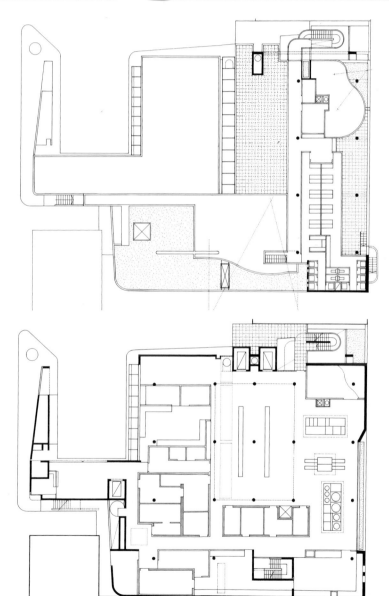

Contextual drawings showing the project's relation to its immediate urban surroundings; its entrances are from the compound and not directly from the street (opposite page top). Axonometric drawing (bottom). Section showing roof lights on the garden terraces. As the building steps up in height, the sun penetrates the various levels. At the top of the building it pours through into the street (top). Plan of roof terraces, offices and workers' club (middle). Site plan and floor plan of functional working area of the kitchen (left).

Pedestrian traffic from the hospital is directed around the loading bays off to one side, defining the edge of the building site. This sets up the route through the kitchen, initiating a promenade on the roof gardens. Arrival (top). Halfway through the walkway (left). Looking back (middle). Detail of the stairs to the plant of the exhaust system. The loggia reveals, through transparency, the modern vocabulary of the building, its open frame permitting the flow of sunshine into the street (opposite page).

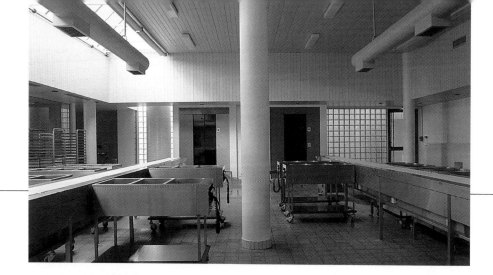

The servant spaces form a wall, which limits two sides of the free plan to contain the square "served" space in which the meals are dished up (top and right). Lounge for the kitchen staff. Its facade of glass blocks gives the program a free and luxurious atmosphere, that of a workers' club (middle). The workers' club overlooks the street (opposite page).

Municipal Child Care Center

MAISON DE L'ENFANCE
TORCY, MARNE-LA-VALLEE, FRANCE

The site of the Maison de l'Enfance is a 45-meter square, which slopes diagonally—with a difference in height of 5 meters between opposite corners. On the top level, a 30-car parking lot is built above the middle level, which is used for public pedestrian access; the lower level is used for service access. The south side is bounded by a 14-meter-wide, dog-legged stairway, which leads to a small square. To the west, the site is separated by an 8-meter-wide passage from a three-story residential block. The entire length of this perimeter opens to a public garden, forming part of the axis of the central public space.

Ciriani's primary aim was to emphasize the angle formed by its north and east sides. The north side runs along urban public space, breaking off at a 90-degree angle to become the east side of the building where the entrance to the center is located. The massing reinforces this angle.

Three levels aligned with the public garden have southerly fenestration, creating a kind of back-lit architecture. Double-height spaces within this volume accentuate the scale of the building with a strongly emphasized frontage. The volume is continued to the east with an unbroken roof line that finally is cut away to reveal an empty space marking the entrance. To anchor the building, this corner is completely opaque at this point. At the end of this great set square, stairs lead to terraces or hanging gardens sloping diagonally in line with the site.

To ensure the necessary unity of the design, the roof slabs are continued vertically down to the ground, becoming the walls of the garden area. The object of this architectonic "ribbon" effect is to make the perimeter walls' continuity a key feature. This rendered concrete ribbon is painted cool gray for necessary sobriety.

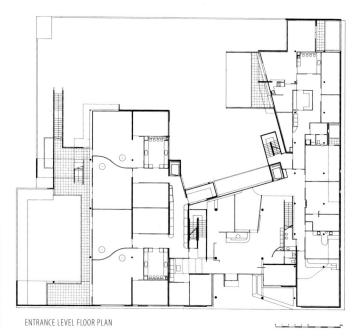

ENTRANCE LEVEL FLOOR PLAN

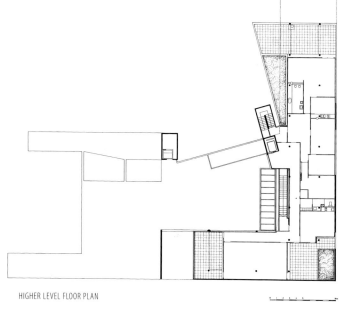

HIGHER LEVEL FLOOR PLAN

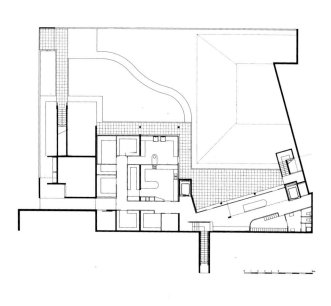

GARDEN LEVEL FLOOR PLAN

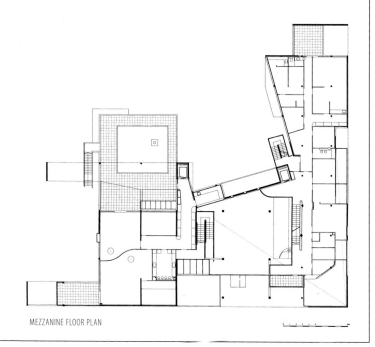

MEZZANINE FLOOR PLAN

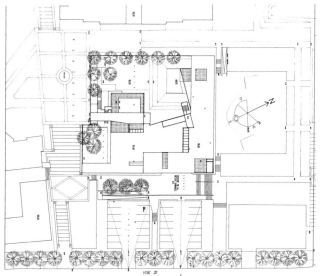

VOIE 25

Overall view of the building from the south. The building opens toward the sun, with a garden and terraces (top). The materialized continuity of bordering planes maintains the unity of the building, whose very complex program can be expressed in all its variety. This formal device enhances the idea of facades as "the protective cloak of society" (left).

The interior ceiling extends out to cover the terrace then plunges downward vertically, at the farthest corner of the lot. Thus the site is controlled and delimited (top and right). Detail of the terrace with the play area for the day-care center (middle). Detail of the facade on the garden side— the central volume (as seen from the west) with the glass of the entrance hall in the background (opposite page).

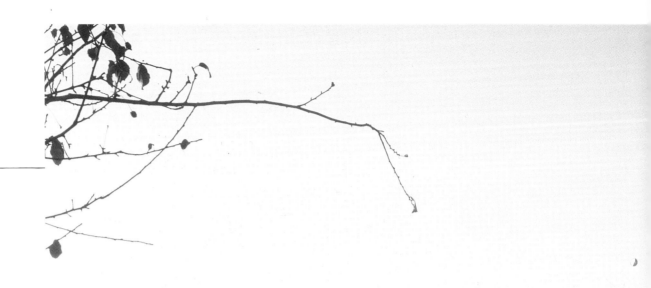

A clear unitary rectangle provides a
strong background for the adjacent
square. A great sense of depth is obtained
by contrasting the enveloping gray
cloak of the facade and the softer pink
wall within, which spreads a warm
atmosphere to the north-facing rooms.
The central double-height entrance hall.
A simple volume, around which unfolds
a complex assemblage of stairs, desk,
seats, rooflights, and cubicles (overleaf).

North wing mezzanine level overlooking the central space (top). Strong contrast between the rather blank perimeter walls of the building's exterior and the strongly lit transparencies of the interior (middle and left). View from the rear wall elevator toward the entrance: showing the "flowing space" (opposite page).

World War 1 Museum

A former stronghold of the northern front, the castle of Péronne was a backdrop for the junction of French and British troops during World War I. The castle's history goes back centuries: Louis XI was held prisoner here in the 1400s. Today, a freeway lies near the town of Péronne, which is a 70-minute drive from Paris. The museum Ciriani designed here did not spring from a collection of weapons and military vehicles, but arose from the notion that the First World War marked a major disruption in the natural course of history. The museum attempts to evoke the reality of the Somme region, where soldiers of many nations battled and died. Thus, the term "historial" was coined to distinguish the museum from other war memorials.

The competition brief emphasized not only the absurdity of the conflict, but also the stubborn faith and belligerence of the parties involved. The idea of "gaps" influenced the architecture: the exhibition was to be structured chronologically into periods of pre-war years, war years, and post-war years, appearing as historical gaps. Trenches could also be viewed as physical gaps.

The periods of the exhibition halls are separated by vertical open spaces that also serve as lighting devices. Its brief called for a space separate from the main galleries where visitors could see portraits of different kinds of people who were involved in the conflict: famous and unknown, living and dead. The provision was later modified during construction—a central portrait gallery explores the relation of the individual to the whole.

Gathered around this central core are halls focusing on the various historical periods. A helix figure is used for the floor plan, appropriate both symbolically and functionally, for it not only creates close views, but also brings in natural light. Barely attached to Péronne's old castle, the new museum establishes a respectful relationship with the historic structure, sharing its simplicity and height. The Historial de la Grande Guerre completes the castle's figure with an elegant west frontage that addresses the landscape and creates a promenade under pilotis along the lake.

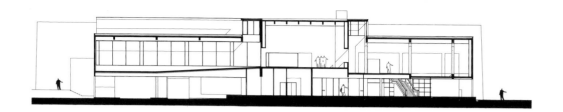

SECTION A NORTH-SOUTH

World War 1 Museum

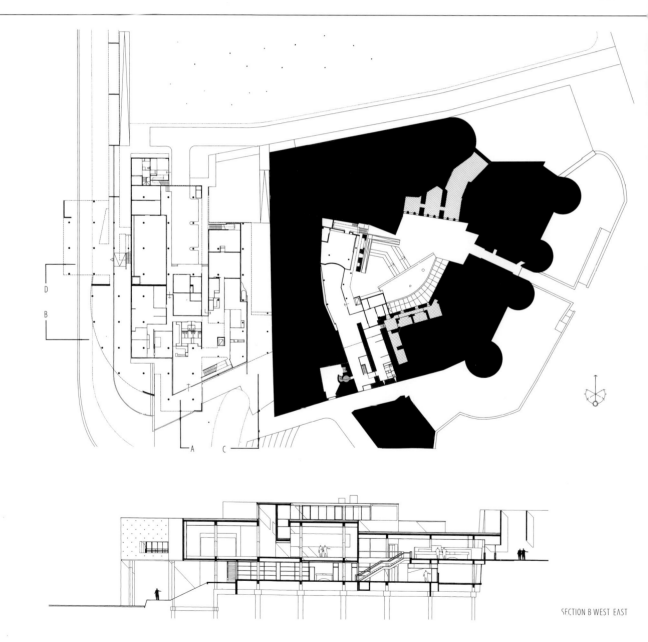

SECTION B WEST EAST

SECTION C SOUTH-NORTH

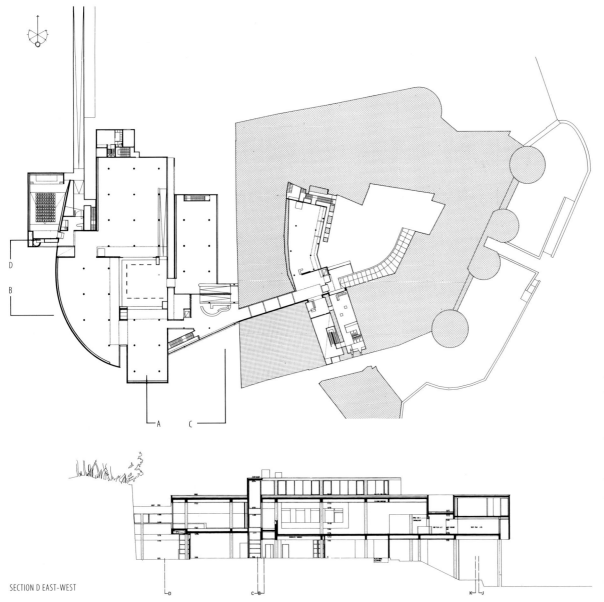

SECTION D EAST-WEST

The upper level: Main museum entrance with the bookstore, temporary exhibition hall and ticket office inside the fortified castle and the museum's five permanent exhibition halls and the auditorium with its own entrance (middle). The lower level: Restaurant and kitchen inside the fortified castle; outside: cafeteria, offices, documentation center, storage, researchers' apartments, maintenance and deliveries (opposite page middle). View of the southern facade. The cylindrical white marble studs inspired by the pattern of white crosses in military cemeteries enlivens the facades while following the sun (overleaf).

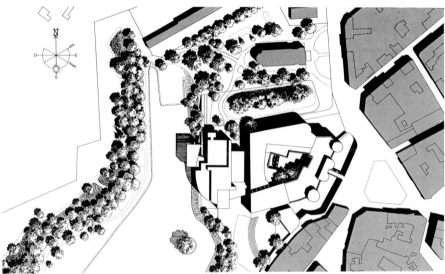

North facade: the building's volumes are fractioned and scaled down in order to combine more easily with its residential surroundings (top). Site plan showing the relation of the city, the castle, the museum, and the lake (middle). Volume of the auditorium over the lake, with its exterior entrance: a ramp stretching fully with the researchers' lodgings as a backdrop (left and opposite page). Overall view of the 1916–1918 hall, where accent was put on speed, progress, and machinery. The natural light that illuminates this room is also reflected toward the adjacent portraits hall (overleaf).

Main entrance (top). Gallery and temporary exhibition hall (middle). The central space, the portrait hall around which the permanent exhibition halls spin (right). The grave calmness of a volume wrapped around itself, the core of the lower level (opposite page).

Archaeological Museum

INSTITUT DE RECHERCHE SUR LA PROVENCE ANTIQUE
ARLES, FRANCE

Situated on a peninsula, this archaeological museum needed to act as an articulation between the old town and the new neighborhoods of Arles. Ciriani's solution was to develop a singular identity for the whole site, composing the landscape in a manner similar to the Campo Santo in Pisa. The adjacent historic Roman circus, because of its size and situation, ensured connection of the site with the old town, leaving Ciriani's firm with the task of designing the museum in a way that would control the remaining buildable space. Since Arles already possesses a historical heritage with forms that derive from the square and the circle, a triangular form was adopted to complete the town's formal repertoire. The pure triangular form is easily recognized; it creates a tension between the new museum and the old Roman circus, and provides complete spatial occupation.

The museum's orientation conditions the degree of opacity of the three walls. The side facing the sun (toward the lock) is totally blank in its outer wall; the one facing the mistral wind toward the Rhône river is a screen that is smooth and glazed; and the third side, facing the Roman circus and old town, is animated by a play of projecting elements and transparencies. Branching out from the entrance hall, two wings form the exhibition spaces that unfold around a central patio and open to the river. The triangular form of the exhibition spaces creates a ring, reducing circulation and facilitating short visits while also

permitting future extension. Because of the size and weight of the items in the museum's collection, the exhibition spaces are at ground level.

Two linear wings (scientific and cultural) border the internal triangle that forms the museum proper. Light is a vital element of the program; natural light is modulated, controlled, or screened by overhangs to create a specific atmosphere in each space. At night, exhibits are illuminated with precise, punctual sources.

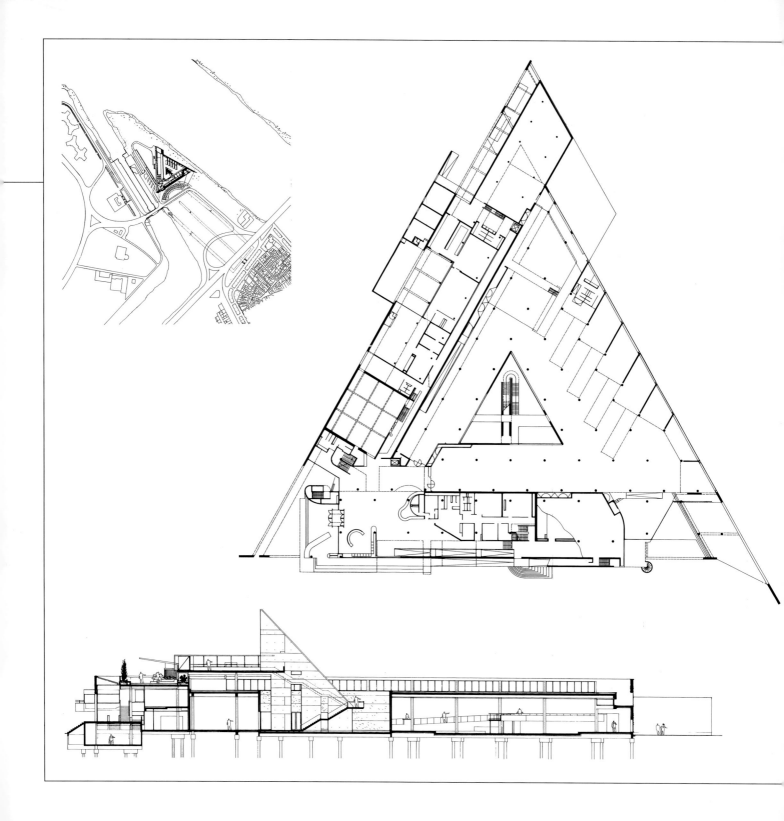

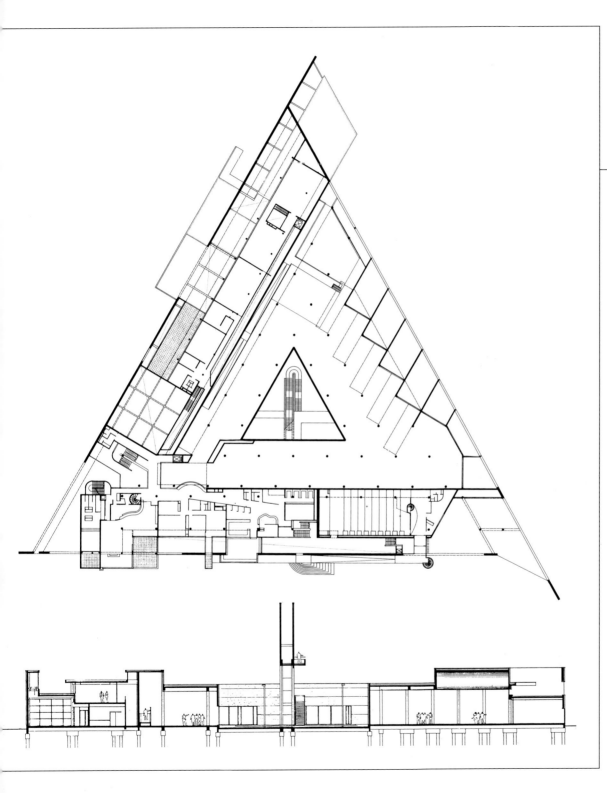

First floor with scientific wing (archaeology school, light-object storage), northeast cultural wing (offices, documentation center and library, cafeteria, and staff rest rooms) (top). Southwest section (left). Site plan, northeast section and ground floor plan with south scientific wing (temporary exhibition hall, laboratories, workshops, heavy-object storage), northeast cultural wing (ticket office, bookshop, school-children educational center, tourist-guide 230-seat auditorium and dressing rooms). Bordered by these two wings and central to the entrance node is the permanent collection exhibition space, which unfurls around an open court and spreads out to fill in that section of the triangle overlooking the third side: the Rhône river (opposite page).

Main facade to the northeast, facing toward the city. From afar, the building positions itself as a gateway to the city as well as a backdrop for the Roman circus. This facade is a horizontal extrusion across the site, screening and framing its symbolic contents (public terrace, director's balcony, library reading room) within. The triangular form is intelligibly concise, yet allows for incidents along its perimeter, with dramatic efficiency at night (overleaf).

Archaeological Museum

View of the northwest facade, facing the river. Facade made from blue glass plates set slightly apart from the concrete walls and spitted-in by flat-headed bolts (right). The plentiful light of the south of France filters through the ceiling and in from the glazed triangular court to illuminate a spatial fluidity. View of the permanent exhibition spaces where clerestory lighting washes off the long red plane to reflect off surfaces opposite and interact with the pristine void of the court (overleaf).

View of the cafeteria toward the main facade with framed views of the historical city (top). Director's office overlooking the double-height gallery (middle). The built-in furniture in *pietra serena* stone animates the entrance lobby (right). View of the entrance area of the gallery parallel to the main facade on the upper level, the cafeteria terrace, and the offices that open onto the upper gallery space (opposite page).

Archaeological Museum

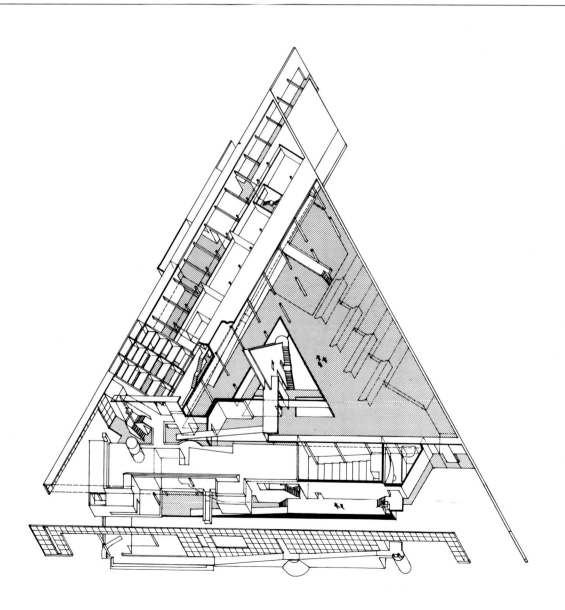

Archaeological displays. View from the platform overlooking the mosaic pit (top). Installations of residential artifacts (middle). Statues from the city's main monuments (bottom). Section through Permanent exhibition area and axonometric view (opposite page).

Marne Social Housing

NOISY-LE-GRAND
MARNE-LA-VALLEE, FRANCE

With this housing project, Ciriani created an urban piece that integrates the planning requirements of the new town of Marne-La-Vallee. The organic link line orthogonally crosses the trunk road on the boundary of the site, proceeds in a straight line across the small block of houses opposite, and finishes at the regional metro station and local shopping center. These simple geometric planes gave rise to the plan of the mass: a T-shaped figure that forms both the structure and the boundary of the space. It consists of two buildings collectively known as Noisy II, and another building, Noisy III:

- A first linear building that functions as an "urban front" in relation to the area it demarcates. As boundary of the piece, this forepart of the project also forms a boulevard with the buildings opposite, one of which was also designed by Ciriani's firm.
- A second linear building that is split and perpendicular to the first building. It contains a central space superimposed on the underground service network and corresponds to the raised organic link line.
- A third building across the street, built a year later.

A large portico at the intersection of the two buildings marks the entrance to the ensemble's domestic element. Together, the linear buildings create simple spatial events that have a tension established by their deep facades and multiple perspectives. The forepart, 180 meters long, represents the whole area by virtue of the disposition of the land, which slopes toward a wide plain. The stepped terraces of the

double building border the pedestrian link leading to other housing in the rear. The scale of the scheme was modeled in terms of its being seen from a distance. The seven living blocks (one of which was punctured to house the entrance porch) are joined by an unobstructed horizontal, regulating the vertical dimension that gives unity to the whole. Since the building faces north, the residential units were planned like round towers joined together; this form, by successive diagonal graduation and angled windows, allows the sun to shine in laterally.

The urban front: the principal linear building is articulated as a representative facade, which both establishes and announces the urban fragment: composed of both a facade and a portal. This main slab first represents the exterior (top), then proclaims and gives entry to the interior (right). Entrances to buildings from southeast park and open spaces (right and opposite page).

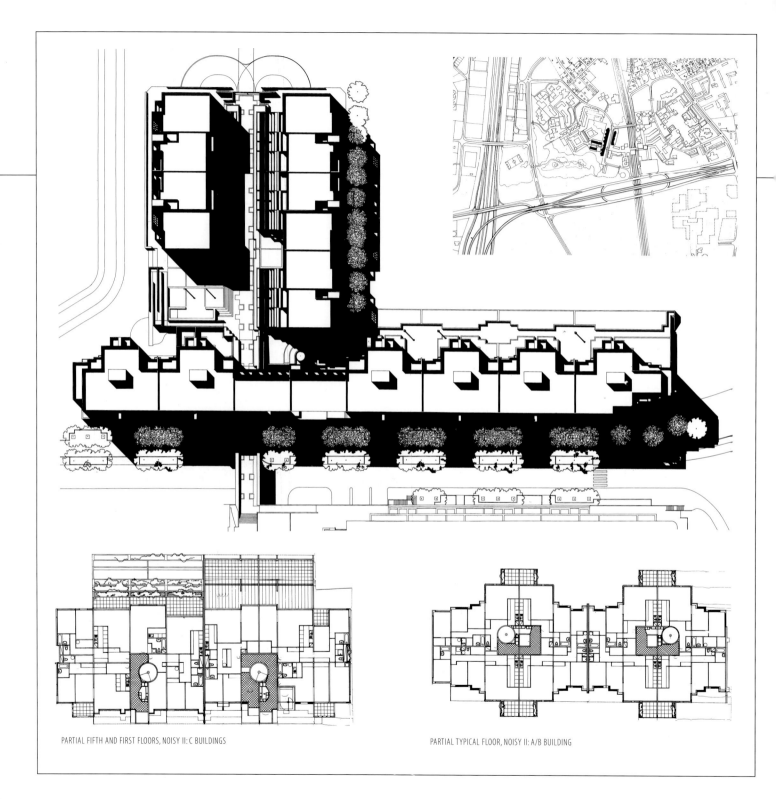

PARTIAL FIFTH AND FIRST FLOORS, NOISY II: C BUILDINGS

PARTIAL TYPICAL FLOOR, NOISY II: A/B BUILDING

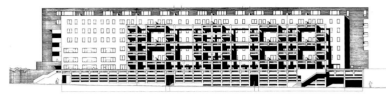

SOUTH ELEVATION

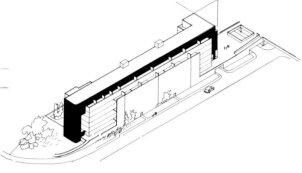

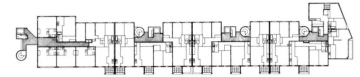

NOISY III: TYPICAL FLOOR PLAN

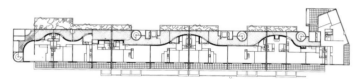

NOISY III: SEVENTH FLOOR

Noisy III linear building, parallel to urban front: Gridded and recessed double-height terraces rise from the footing (garage). The small units of the last floor permit a volume to rejoin the vertical sculptural volume of circulation at one end of the building (right) to the front. This is the dominant image of the building, the hole being covered with the same red tiles as the opposing building (opposite page).

Saint-Denis Social Housing and Facility

LA COURDANGLE
SAINT-DENIS, FRANCE

In the town of Saint-Denis, north of Paris, Ciriani's firm was asked to design a housing facility on a lot in a new urban development grafted to the ancient hierarchy of closely ordered streets. To the north is an incongruous collection of 11- to 18-story-high housing blocks. The site is bordered by two types of streets: To the south is rue Auguste-Poullain, the main axis, 14 meters wide with a 95-meter frontage; to the east is rue Jean-Mermoz, 10 meters wide with an 80-meter frontage.

This project takes advantage of two of the statutory town planning regulations. The first is a height limit of seven stories, allowing the building to be seen from a large open space opposite the rue Auguste-Poullain frontage, which is used as a fairground. Also, the new building had to border the two existing streets.

The program called for 130 apartments, mainly small; 230 underground parking spaces; and a municipal day care center for 60 children from early infancy to two years of age. The housing program imposed a very strict building rationalization, justifying the use of a single-size grid. The 5.6-meter grid, already tried in the firm's Marne housing project, was used and extended vertically. In the daycare facility, situated on the ground floor of a four-story building, Ciriani methodically worked on spatial continuity and the placing of volumes to move natural light through transparencies. At the corner of rue Jean-Mermoz, this long building is met by a second one, and their intersection generates a central space that reinforces the buildings' unity.

The envelope of La Courdangle is made of planes whose differences are emphasized by the use of color. The foremost plane is in white concrete; the wall (the internal boundary of the facade space) has strips of red tiles and concrete. The planes become autonomous through the use of blue for the volumes they contain, which are the third component of the envelope. These volumes move within the thickness of the frontal space and, through color, reassert their reference to cubism and abstraction.

The seven-story building with its striped cladding and geometric frieze rises above the chaos of the neighboring streets and forms a corner in this otherwise unstructured space (top). Courdangle street floor (right). By creating a visually strong plane of geometrical precision the project is inspired by the still-life composition device: Transformed into a picture plane, the various autonomous free-standing buildings as well as the high-rises are integrated into a new harmonious urban setting (opposite page). Axonometric of the block with the project at its southeast corner (opposite page middle).

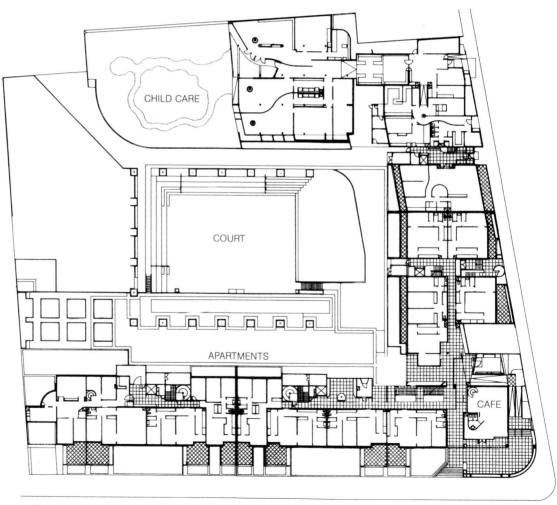

CHILD CARE

COURT

APARTMENTS

CAFE

COUR D'ANGLE: STREET FLOOR

N↑ ⊢——⊣ 20'/6m

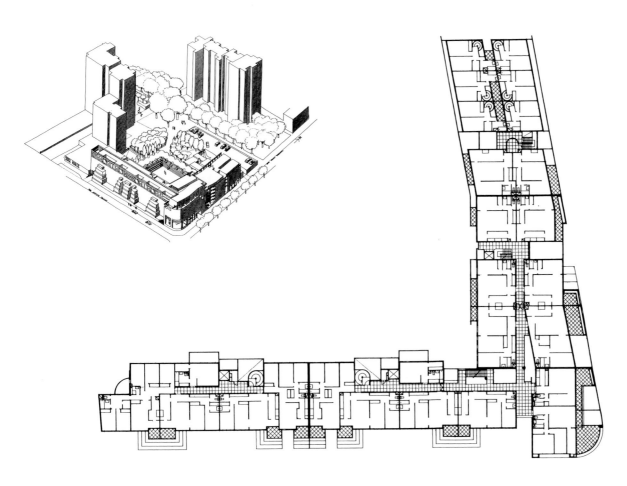

TYPICAL FLOOR PLAN (FLOORS 1 TO 5)

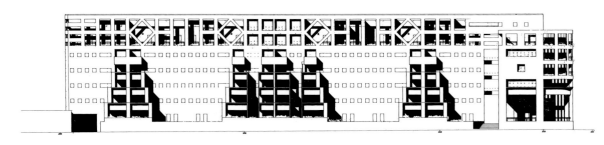

SOUTH ELEVATION

The inside is a pure, right-angled figure containing a perfectly defined square space. The residential quality is increased by the greenery (top). The presence of a low horizontal child-care center bordering the north side of the square (right). The layering of the facades facilitates the articulation of the decreasing volumes as well as lodging the apartments' exterior spaces. The blue plane permits the building to dissolve itself into the sky (opposite page).

Children's play areas with morphologically designed doors: "to see the child is to protect him" (top and middle). The director's office fully glazed in order to participate completely in the life of the center (left). The whole child-care center project is organized around a unique central route whose transparency puts the garden play areas (at farthest end) in visual contact with the entrance lobby (in the foreground) (opposite page).

Evry Social Housing

ZAC DU CANAL
EVRY-COURCOURONNES, FRANCE

In the Zac du Canal district of the new town of Evry, a 300-meter linear rainwater reservoir runs east to west. On the far side, Ciriani's firm was given a building lot whose urban significance was heightened by the public right of way linking the district to the neighboring park to the east. The building was supposed to outrange its immediate surroundings and at the same time incorporate an urban gate in its center.

While the frontage of the building, overlooking the canal, is the dominant aspect, it was essential that the project be given a uniform architectonic treatment on all sides to ensure overall unity. From its six different levels, the building dominates the two- to three-story structures along the canal.

Addressing the volumetric aspects of the building to establish an immediate visual identity, Ciriani first opted for a portico that would conform to the town's requirements and also stem from the morphology of the area. The architect then gave the individual apartments a straightforward collective treatment, concentrating on ridge-roofing and the essential supports for the formal work on the building as a whole. The ridge-roofing had to be reinforced in order to address the vast expanse in front. The portico reference was then replaced by a suggestion of a raised arcade. To increase the building's impact on its surroundings, Ciriani also enhanced the shape of the upper floors to produce the effect of an inverted pyramid.

The requirements imposed by the local authorities were combined with the client's demands: natural light in all kitchens and bathrooms, and extended living areas as compared with the usual apartments in this type of social housing. The architect added outdoor terraces as another necessity. The constraints gave way to a large variety of apartment types and differentiated terraces that maximize sunlight.

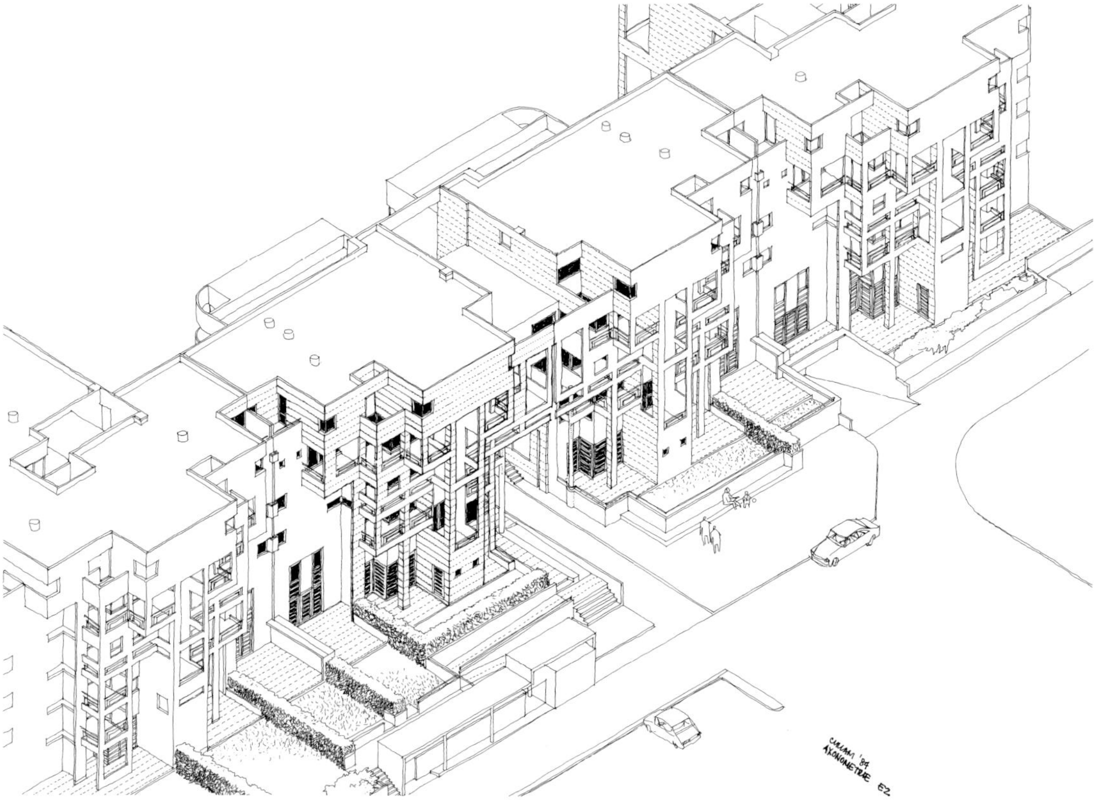
'84
AXONOMETRIE E2

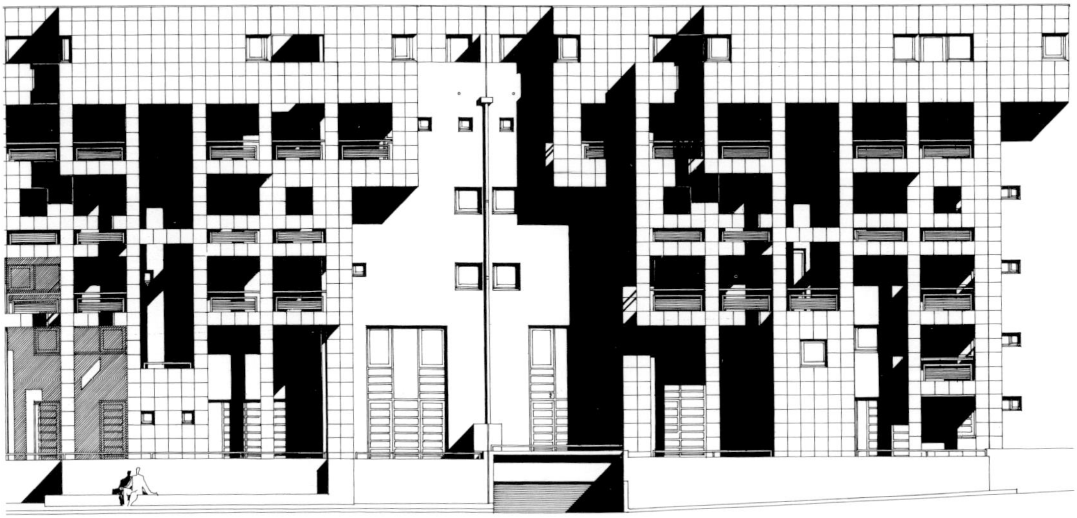

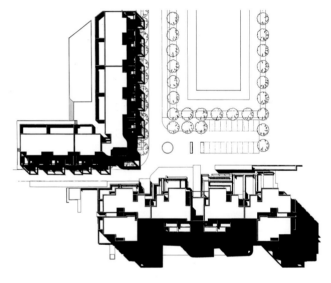

The east (rear) facade emphasizes the formal identity of types. The formal calmness of volumes open to the residential garden contiguous to the neighboring park (top and left). The west front is the backdrop to a 300-meter-long canal. More weight is put into the upper volumes in order that the building may address the significant perspective over the canal. The facade's inverted pyramid defies the laws of gravity, yet it is quite light. It is in fact a "captive" space (overleaf).

TYPICAL FLOOR (2ND & 3RD FLOORS)

FIRST FLOOR

STREET FLOOR

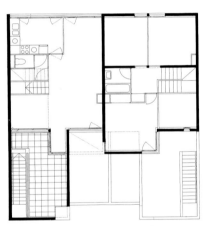

PLAN OF LOWER AND UPPER FLOOR OF HOUSE

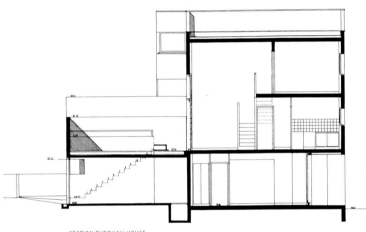

SECTION THROUGH HOUSE

Row houses bordering the canal, behind the central hospital (top). Garages on the ground floor, terraces, the volume of the double-height living room prolongs itself into the terrace, which also articulates the individual access stairs (left).

Lognes Social Housing and Facility

ZAC DU SEGRAIS, LOGNES
MARNE-LA-VALLEE, FRANCE

This project lies at the edge of a development in the Lognes district of the new town of Marne-la-Vallee, opposite a protective embankment for the nearby freeway. This raised area is now a sports and leisure park.

The southerly crescent shape designed by the town planners is intersected in the middle by an access road to the neighborhood coming from the park and the freeway. Ciriani's firm decided to build on three parallel vertical levels:

- The first level adapts itself to the perimeter of the land; a lattice level's height corresponds with that of the upper terrace level of the park, the ground floor functions as a commercial arcade. A superimposed terrace treatment, simulating wings torn away from the first grid, serves the purpose of appearing to bring together the two sides of the central axis.
- The second level is straight, delineating the living area of the apartments behind the grid. Terraced balconies bridge the gap between the first and second levels.
- The third component consists of two recessed upper levels that have a pronounced curve to make them more autonomous. These elements have the effect of reaching out to meet their counterpart on the other side of the road, virtually breaching the gap to close the semicircle. They also anchor the spaces in the center behind the lattice, their opaque stability making it possible for the first level to blend with the space in front.

Two porches face each other at angles, forming an access area for the residential parts of the buildings. From this area spring the vertical circulations of the entrance halls. The buildings are crowned with a rooftop *maisonette* typology, with the apartments having access from a deck overlooking the whole new town.

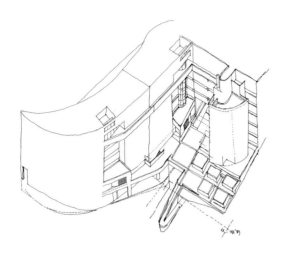

AXONOMETRIC FROM GARDEN SIDE

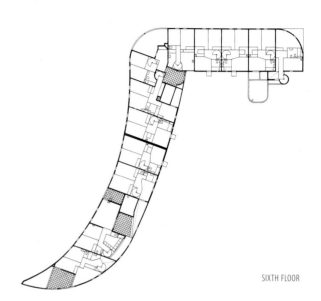

SIXTH FLOOR

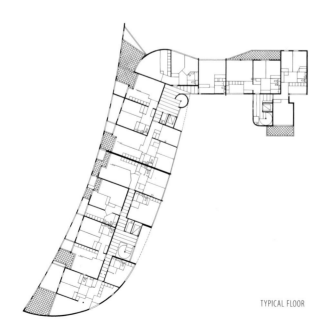

TYPICAL FLOOR

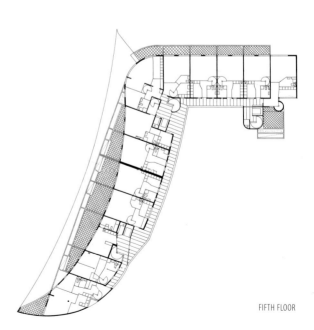

FIFTH FLOOR

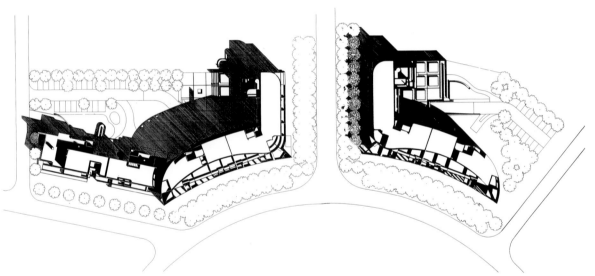

Aerial view of the site; the linear structure to the right (in background) is the railroad viaduct (top). Rear north-facing facade to residential area opening into garden and lake. The apparent massiveness was needed in order to anchor the building (rear).

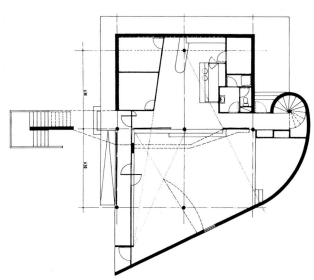

This small community center is used for collective activities ranging from youth clubs to weddings or anniversaries. Small rooms (top and right) open into bigger ones in a fluid way assisted by the use of color and light around the themes of reflection, rough and glossy, bright and dark, thus creating a unified pictorial sequence (opposite page).

Establishing a serene order: these six-story buildings are perceived at two scales, that of the monumental curve understood in its entirety, and the more intimate scale perceived by a pedestrian who wanders from light to shadow beneath its generous loggia, or goes around to the more informal rear facade crowned by a street-in-the-air that serves as access to the duplexes on the top floors (middle). The entrance to the buildings is through two porches facing each other. The whole building is making an effort to enhance the entrance: a residential threshold (top). The glazed circulation systems to the north of the five-story building (left).

Charcot Social Housing and Shops

RUE DU CHEVALERET
PARIS, FRANCE

Ciriani's Charcot housing project seeks to improve Parisian residential living space, to make it become the matrix of urban form. Whereas a new city presents the enormous responsibility of creating the city itself, a collective framework in which to locate individuality, in Paris, the city already exists with clear, consolidated, compulsory rules. Entrances and shops are on the ground floor and are within horizontal city planning norms, and above are volumetric limitations and recessed facades.

In the midst of these constraints, a certain urban regularity emerges in Paris that places value on the subtle individuality of each building. This is a concept Ciriani thinks noteworthy: the greater the simplicity, the more varied and pleasing the result. He believes that the most desirable approach to new construction in a city such as Paris is not to contradict the rules handed down from past centuries, nor to passively accept them. Instead, architects should face the challenge of maintaining the same level of simplicity and pertinence.

Ciriani's commitment to this approach is evident in this project. The apartments are duplexes, like a series of *petites villas*. On the facade, each is contained in a square zone 5.6 meters wide and two stories high. This rationalist, direct aspect of the design defines an order that is related to the structure, creating rapport between the two scales, that of the edifice and that of the dwelling. The grid is the unifying

factor of the entire edifice. Calm and silent, it is rigorous and contains a free, individual form. Certain residential elements have been incorporated, such as balconies, louvered shutters, and bow windows.

On the side of the building, given that rue Charcot is on a hill, the levels are staggered toward the top. This avoids a visual flattening of the ground floor, making it possible to break up the uniformity while at the same time referring to a traditional element of French architecture, the mezzanine.

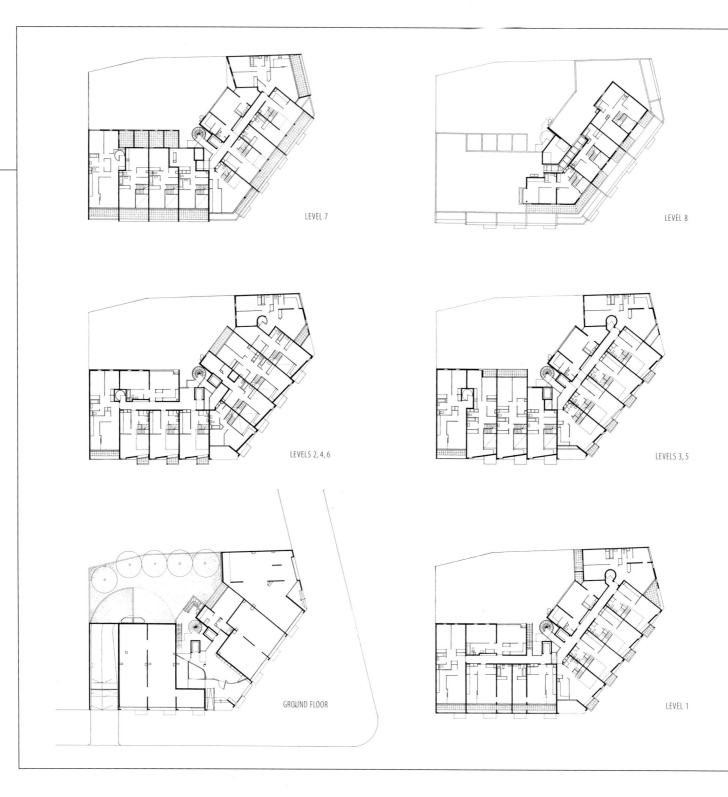

LEVEL 7

LEVEL 8

LEVELS 2, 4, 6

LEVELS 3, 5

GROUND FLOOR

LEVEL 1

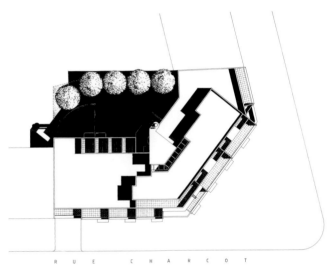

R U E   C H A R C O T

Overall view in its current Parisian setting. The building's scale addresses the future street giving access to the French National Library (top). View of the entrance and atrium (left).

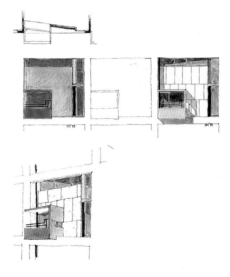

The recessed upper floors follow Parisian roofline regulations (top). The grid is rigorous and contains a free individual form. Into it, certain residential signs have been incorporated, like the balcony, the louvered shutters and the bow windows (middle). View of the corner showing the vertical articulation of both the staggering duplexes (split relation) and the entrance, which is located in the indentation of the corner cutting the facade up to the top. This large vertical element permits staggered levels toward the top on the left side adapting to the sloping site (left).

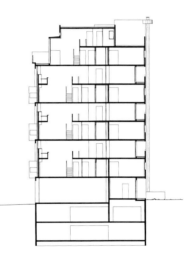

View of the two-story balcony leading to the apartments: the balconies face each other across a central windowed space. The top two floors duplex with terraced balconies, respecting the Parisian rooftop regulations (top). Entrance, kitchen, and living areas in the lower level (middle and opposite page). Master bedroom with working space overlooking the double-height living-room and terrace (bottom).

Bercy Social Housing and Shops

RUE DE L'AUBRAC
PARIS, FRANCE

In this Paris urban model it was stipulated that coherent urban lots be assigned to architects. Ciriani's firm was asked to design two linear buildings on either side of a 12-meter-wide pedestrian pathway linking the rue de Lamy to the new Bercy park to the southwest. The architect placed the main entrances to his buildings on this footpath.

Facing the park, Ciriani proposed two types of apartments. One type, extensively glazed, opens to a continuous balcony every two stories. The other, equally open to the balcony, uses it as part of an urban loggia common to the adjacent building. This allowed Ciriani to incorporate the neighboring low-rises to the project's lateral blank walls.

The long volumes were divided into two parts:
- The duplex apartments overlook the park. Some of these also are situated over a pedestrian pathway, with their frontage diagonally oriented—like fish gills—so they face the park views. The larger three- to five-bedroom apartments are in this part of the building.
- Overlooking the rue de Lamy, the architect placed the volume that responds to the client's program requirements of smaller one-level apartments structured vertically. The studios, albeit situated in the rear, are open to the park through the urban loggias. The one-bedroom apartments are L-shaped, sur-rounding a terrace opening to the street, and the two-bedroom apartments are either parallel to the pedestrian pathway or open on two sides.

The buildings were designed to successfully incorporate the urban cleft imposed by the plan. Ciriani's vision included 3.5-meter cantilevers projecting from the continuous balconies, but this part of the firm's proposal did not receive planning approval. The cantilevers would have allowed the architect to virtually close the space and thus evoke the "park gate" typology—a much-appreciated residential feature of the Parisian Parc Monceau—in a contemporary manner.

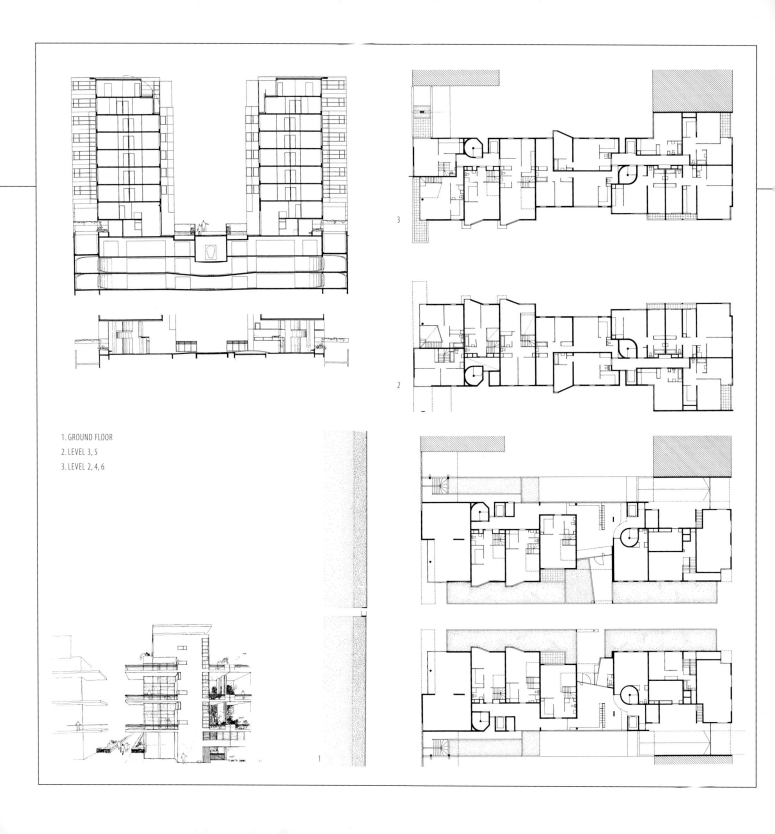

1. GROUND FLOOR
2. LEVEL 3, 5
3. LEVEL 2, 4, 6

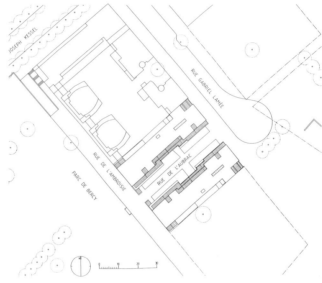

The two recessed floors make the pedestrian street wider in the center part (top). Double-height glass walls represent the duplexes facing the park while lateral duplexes seek their views toward the green space (middle). The double height and full width of the building permits the entrance lobby of one building to create a continuously broad space perpendicular to the pedestrian route (overleaf).

The double height and full width of the building permits the entrance lobby of one building to create a continuously broad space perpendicular to the pedestrian route (top). Interior view of the lateral duplexes showing the glazed working space off the master bedroom and the lateral shift of the lower floor toward the park (middle). Interior views of the park-front duplex (left and opposite page).

Colombes Social Housing Facility and Shops

AVENUE DE STALINGRAD
COLOMBES, FRANCE

Situated northwest of Paris, not far from the A86 orbital motorway, the town of Colombes once had a composite quarter whose torn urban fabric cried out for repair. A section of this quarter was designated for redevelopment: a triangular lot on the corner of two main roads, inserted between a densely constructed area of small detached houses and an expanse of undeveloped terrain dotted with depressing high-rise apartment blocks built in the 1960s. The lot contained an eight-story apartment building that was to remain.

The basic aim of the project was easily stated: to use new buildings to bring unity to this part of the city by creating a gentle progression of scale between the widely differing original buildings—a sort of urban pacification. When translated into spatial language, this meant defining three levels in the area.

The lowest level comprises small detached family houses, each with a one-and-a-half-story living room and an upper floor, designed to blend with the existing low-rise neighborhood. These new houses built in straight lines give the street a distinctive identity and mark the start of a volumetric progression that increases in height as the triangular site gradually broadens. The intermediate level is composed of the *hotel particulier* or "plot" type, having the maximum feasible height for walk-up buildings. The buildings are joined by lateral terraces that create the transparency needed to bring light and air to the interior of the block. The terraces also coherently extend space toward the adjacent gardens of the detached houses to the rear.

The highest level comprises typologies of small two- or three-bedroom linear apartments with windows on two sides, or only one side when facing the garden, plus duplex apartments overlooking two sides.

The vertical building exploits the corner site by being detached, like a campanile marking the entrance to a town. This also made it possible to open the *immeuble-villas* on three sides, a step toward an elevated-house type.

Colombes Social Housing
Facility and Shops

PHOTO, OPPOSITE TOP   PHOTO, OPPOSITE CENTER

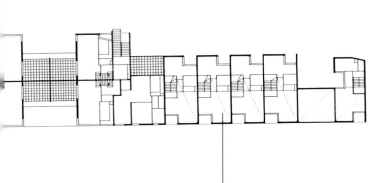

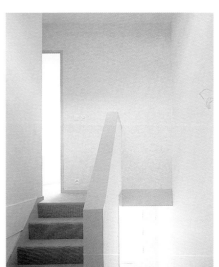

PHOTO, BOTTOM

The vertical space of the three-story-high apartments. This type is used to articulate two different heights of buildings (top). The horizontal window of the duplexes contrast with the two-story height space with an upper balcony (middle). The split-level system of the two-and-a-half level row houses (left). The necessary volumetric progression in order to integrate an eight-floor existing building as well as two-story neighboring houses (opposite page).

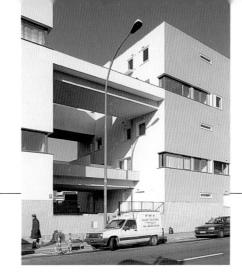

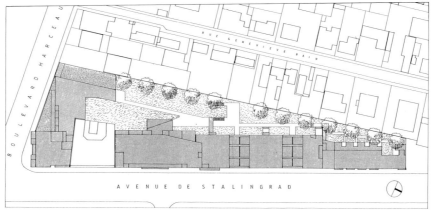

The *hôtel particulier* type. Houses with terraces in between the buildings, creating transparencies between the street and the inner garden, thus allowing the neighboring freestanding houses to breathe through (top and left). Urban presence of the corner building acting as pivot to anchor the site. It is composed of very comfortable duplexes opened to three sides (opposite page).

The Hague Apartment Building

DEDEMSVAARTWEG
THE HAGUE, THE NETHERLANDS

To celebrate its 200,000th housing unit, the City of The Hague and the Federation of Hague Housing Corporations decided to build a special housing estate in which architects from various countries were invited to express their visions. Officially launched in 1989, this housing exhibition was named Stichting Woning-bouwfestival 200.000ste Woning Dedemsvaartweg.

The Morgenstond area, to the southwest of the city and near Zuider park, is structured by strips of green, one of which was crossed at one point by a vacant strip of land laid bare for a freeway that was never built. The plan of the estate was commissioned to the Rotterdam-based Oma, who divided the strip into three sectors. To the north are one-floor houses called "confettis"; in the middle, three-story urban villas; and situated in the south are four 10-story housing towers, one of which was commissioned to Ciriani's office.

The building's compactness is due to the requirements of the program, and its austerity and rigor were dictated by a strict budget. Two parallel slabs, covered with white and green enamel, leave an empty strip in the middle. The slabs are linked by a central vertical and horizontal circulation system that has been left open on nine levels. At each landing, a bridge leads on both sides to two adjacent terraces. The bridges give a second access to the two-bedroom apartments situated at the angles and disposing of three orientations (Dutch regulations call for two entrances to each apartment, one of which must be exterior). On the ground and first floors, Ciriani placed duplex apartments that open to a garden and to the entrance hall and storerooms for bicycles and baby carriages in the core of the building. The top floor is occupied by two penthouses with large roof gardens.

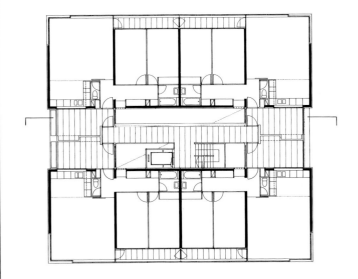

TYPICAL FLOOR PLAN

TOP FLOOR PLAN

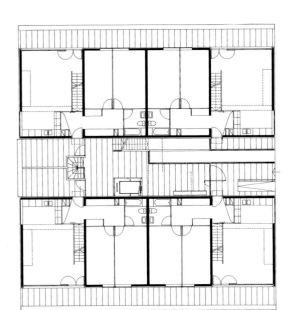

GROUND FLOOR PLAN

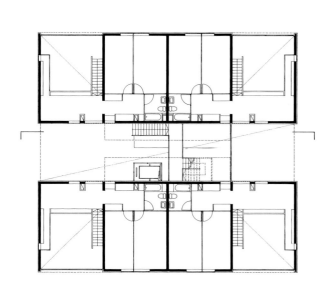

FIRST FLOOR PLAN

At night the building's logic of volumes and voids is clearly expressed. The corner windows of the living rooms create a virtual plane of light layered against the colorful red and blue verticalities of the building (left). The two slick vertical slabs united by the lateral terraces are built over two stories of ground level units with private gardens and topped by two penthouse apartments (opposite page).

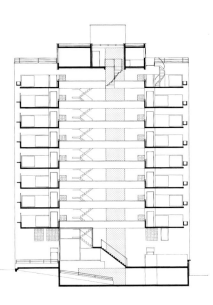

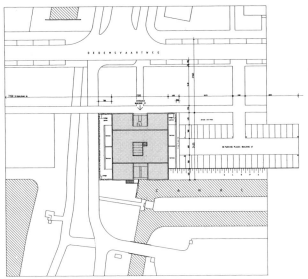

The central core of the building is a void occupied by the pedestrian bridges and glazed elevator (top) and an open vertical staircase (left). Entrance level of interior atrium with private access to ground floor duplexes (opposite page).

In Progress ▶

Groningen Towers

Following a period in which Ciriani sought an articulation within the traditional city, he decided to progress with his typological work with this project, his first Dutch building. His goal was to get back to the essence of architecture—space and form—by defining a prototypical building that would be the vehicle for new spatiality. This prototype would avoid the current trend of allowing projects to be defined by their detailing or materials, such as structural glazing and exposed structures.

Ciriani's research for the past twelve years has explored, among other things, the idea of an urban elevated ground space by reproducing the conditions of a ground floor up in the air. This artificial ground space is sufficiently wide, protected by its limits to ensure that the inhabitants are not face-to-face with empty space. Gaining horizontals by height means making artificial ground, and Ciriani's Groningen project develops the horizontal plane to its extreme possibilities.

All of the architect's work in the Netherlands consists of envelopes for people to live in, relating with the external artificial ground. The root—the archetype—is Corbusier's *immeuble-villa* that carries within itself its own ground space. Ciriani's interpretation, however, involves a transformation of scale. Artificial ground space no longer is in relationship with a single cell, but with a mass of cells. It claims urban status.

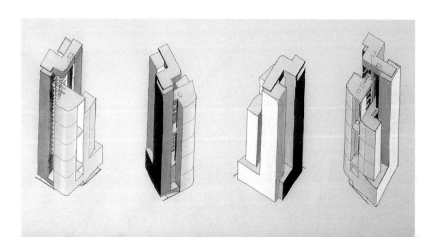

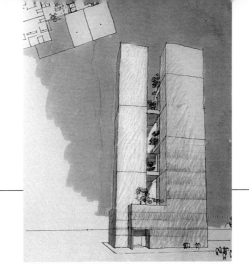

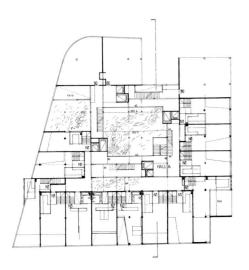

FLOORS 2, 3, 4

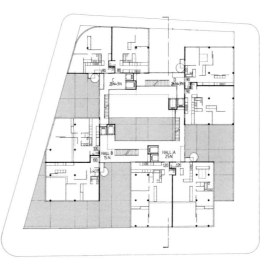

TYPICAL FLOOR PLAN

Four towers linked by suspended gardens every five floors, alternatively suspended over each other every ten floors, decrease in height from thirty stories to twenty to let the south sun into the central core. The city height (around four stories) constitutes the unitary base for the four towers.

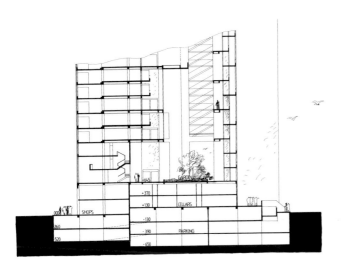

The symbolic and visual value of the skyscraper is enhanced by the use of color. The idea of a building "following the sun" is fostered by the whiteness of the south volume (top). The dark black verticality of the northern volume (middle and opposite page) is starkly contrasted by the blank yellow verticality (left).

Nijmegen Towers

The city of Nijmegen, with a population of 145,000 and a 20,000-student university, shares with the city of Arnhem a vast plain occupied by the busy river Waal. Parallel to the river front is the base of a triangular-shaped site whose second and third sides contrast: The side to the southeast is very strongly felt because of an elevated railway track, and the other is poorly defined by sad low-rise housing schemes.

Ciriani's high-rise will be the vertical landmark of Nijmegen's new developing west area and harbor. The project will establish an identity and make visual and functional connections with the central core, while also seeking to enliven the immediate environment through the quality of its dwellings and gardens.

The building is a linear figure produced by four square towers joined together by their diagonals in plan and revealing in elevation a structure of stepped volumes twenty to thirty stories high, from the river up. These towers are grounded to the site by a right-angled podium fostering continual movement between the vertical and the horizontal. This diagonally sustained shape looks different from each of its four sides, thus providing a good urban orientation device. The hanging gardens are used to screen railroad noise as well as to relate to the city's park on the other side of the track, giving the historical center the image of a vertical garden. From the other side, the buildings, which tower over the country-side far beyond, will look more abstract, their colors contributing to their strong painterly image.

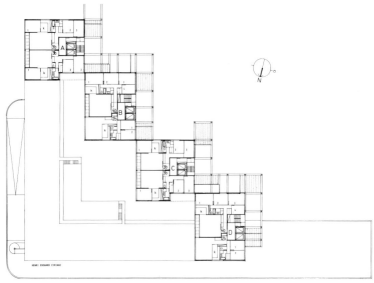

HENRI EDOUARD CIRIANI

Views of the model, showing the final garden structure facing south (opposite page); the towers seen as parallels to the railroad (top) and seen from the river (left). Drawings of the first project, with the screen of gardens proposed in a more autonomous way. West (top left), northwest (top right), east (bottom left), and south (bottom right) perspectives (overleaf).

OUEST

NI 01
4

NORD-OUEST

EST

NI 01
1

SUD

NI 01
5

Appendix ▶

List of Works and Credits

HOSPITAL KITCHEN
66 SAINT ANTOINE HOSPITAL, RUE DE CÎTEAUX, PARIS XII
1981–1985, Paris, France
Client: Assistance Publique
Project Team: Henri Ciriani with Jacky Nicolas
Structural Engineers: J. Gillant, Befs
Electrical Engineer: Seef
Mechanical Engineer and kitchen consultant: Sepa
Contractor: Setb
Photographers: Stéphane Couturier, Christian Devillers, Marcela Espejo,
Jean-Marie Monthiers, Delde von Schaewen

MUNICIPAL CHILD CARE CENTER
MAISON DE L'ENFANCE
8, RUE PIERRE-MENDES-FRANCE AT TORCY
1986–1989, Marne-La-Vallee, France
Client: San de Marne-La-Vallee
Project Team: Henri Ciriani with Jacky Nicolas and Richard Doorly
Engineers: Igm
Contractor: Heulin
Photographers: Stéphane Couturier, Christian Devillers, Jean-Marie Monthiers

WORLD WAR 1 MUSEUM
HISTORIAL DE LA GRANDE GUERRE, PLACE DU CHATEAU
1987–1992, Péronne, France
Client: Conseil General de la Somme
Project Team: Henri Ciriani with Jean-Claude Laisné and Jacky Nicolas,
Nathalie du Luart, Olivier Abriat, Jean Pierre Crousse, Michel Nadorp
Structural Engineer: Marc Mimram
Electrical Engineer: Cegef
Mechanical Engineer: Inex
Contractor: Léon Grosse
Photographer: Jean-Marie Monthiers

ARCHAEOLOGICAL MUSEUM
INSTITUT DE RECHERCHE SUR LA PROVENCE ANTIQUE,
PRESQU'ÎLE DU CIRQUE ROMAIN
1983–1995, Arles, France
Client: City of Arles
Project Team: Henri Ciriani with Jacky Nicolas, Jacques Bajolle and Michel Dayot,
Richard Doorly, Jean Pierre Crousse, Nathalie du Luart, Olivier Abriat,
Anne Sobotta, Laurent Tournié, Malcolm Nouvel, Miguel Macian, Hérve Dubois,
Laurent Scatola, Dominique Neves
Structural Engineers: Scobat, Cesba
Electrical Engineer: Scobat, Optima
Mechanical Engineer: Inex
Contractors: Spie-Mediterranee, Héritier, Amans, Ateliers Saint Jacques, Roiret
Photographer: Jean-Marie Monthiers

MARNE SOCIAL HOUSING
RUE DE LA BUTTE VERTE, NOISY-LE-GRAND
1975–1981, Marne-La-Vallee, France
Clients: Foyer du Fonctionnaire et de la Famille and Interprofessionnelle de la
Région Parisienne
Project Team: Henri Ciriani with Vincent Sabatier
Structural Engineers: Oth and Cerc
Mechanical & Electrical Engineers: Oth
Contractor: Setb and Bouygues
Photographers: Philippe Chair, Michel Desjardins, Marcela Espejo, Yves Lion,
Claire Robinson

SAINT-DENIS SOCIAL HOUSING & FACILITY
LA COURDANGLE, 22, RUE AUGUSTE-POULLAIN, 23, RUE JEAN-MERMOZ
1978–1983, Saint-Denis, France
Clients: Le Logement Dionysien and the City of Saint-Denis
Project Team: Henri Ciriani with David Mangin, Vincent Sabatier, Jacky Nicolas
Structural Engineers: Cerc, Lucien Filossi
Mechanical Engineer: Lafi
Contractors: Tassoni, Ecoba, Scgd, Sgm
Photographers: Philippe Chair, Michel Desjardins, Marcela Espejo

EVRY SOCIAL HOUSING
ZAC DU CANAL, RUE DE LA MARE DIACRE, EVRY-COURCOURONNES
1981–1986, Evry, France
Client: La Sabliere
Project Team: Henri Ciriani with Michel Dayot & Jacques Garcin, Jacky Nicolas
Structural Engineer: Lucien Filossi
Electrical Engineer: Secie
Mechanical Engineer: Lafi
Contractor: Smctp
Photographer: Christian Devillers

LOGNES SOCIAL HOUSING & FACILITY
61–69, BOULEVARD DU SEGRAIS, LOGNES
13, RUE GIUSEPPE VERDI, LOGNES
BOULEVARD DU SEGRAIS
1982–1987, Marne-La-Vallee, France
Clients: Société Française des Habitations Economiques, Société Française de Credit
Immobilier and Epamarne
Project Team: Henri Ciriani with Richard Henriot and Jacques Garcin, Dominique
Delord-Garcin, Michel Dayot, Jacky Nicolas
Structural Engineer: Lucien Filossi
Electrical Engineer: Scobat
Mechanical Engineer: Lafi
Contractor: Setb
Photographers: Stéphane Couturier, Christian Devillers, Richard Henriot

CHARCOT SOCIAL HOUSING & SHOPS
127, RUE DU CHEVALERET, PARIS XIII
1987–1991, Paris, France
Client: La Sabliere
Project Team: Henri Ciriani with Jean-Pierre Crousse and Miguel Macian, Jean-Claude Laisne
Structural Engineer: Scobat
Mechanical Engineer: Iratome
Contractor: Sicra
Photographers: Stéphane Couturier, Jean-Marie Monthiers

BERCY SOCIAL HOUSING & SHOPS
5 & 6, RUE DE L'AUBRAC, PARIS XII
1991–1994, Paris, France
Client: Opac de Paris
Project Team: Henri Ciriani with Jean Pierre Crousse and Richard Doorly,
Miguel Macian, Laurent Tournié, Michel Nadorp
Engineers: Scobat
Contractor: Gtm Btp
Photographer: Jean-Marie Monthiers

COLOMBES SOCIAL HOUSING FACILITY & SHOPS
77–91, AVENUE DE STALINGRAD, COLOMBES
1992–1995, Colombes, France
Client: Semco
Project Team: Henri Ciriani with Jean Pierre Crousse and Olivier Abriat,
Malcolm Nouvel, Enrique Santillana, Michel Nadorp, Laurent Scatola
Engineers: Scobat
Contractor: Dumez
Photographer: Jean-Marie Monthiers

THE HAGUE APARTMENT BUILDING
DEDEMSVAARTWEG 1125–1201, MORGENSTOND
1990–1995, the Hague, Holland
Client: Geerlings Vastgoed B.V.
Project Team: Henri Ciriani with Jean Pierre Crousse and Olivier Abriat,
Michel Nadorp, Jacky Nicolas
Electrical Engineer: van der Niet
Mechanical Engineer: Stagro
Contractor: Maarsens Bouwbedrifj B.V.
Photographer: Jean-Marie Monthiers

GRONINGEN TOWERS
WINSCHOTERKADE, GRONINGEN
1988–1990, Groningen, Holland
Client: Geerlings Vastgoed B.V.
Project Team: Henri Ciriani with Jean-Claude Laisne
Structural Engineer: Dijkhuis

NIJMEGEN TOWERS
WAALHAVEN, NIJMEGEN, HOLLAND
1989–1990, Nijmegen, Holland
Client: Geerlings Vastgoed B.V.
Project Team: Henri Ciriani with Michel Nadorp
Structural Engineer: Dijkhuis
Model Photographer: Jean-Marie Monthiers

Henri Ciriani (1) surrounded by part of the numerous staff that has
worked in the Paris office through the years: Vincent Sabatier (2), Isabel
Calderon (3), Marcelle Ciriani (4), Jurg Heuberger (5), Laura Ciriani (6),
Chun-Ko Koon (7), Jacky Nicolas (8), Jean-François Chenais (9), Olivier
Arene (10), Gilles Margot-Duclot (11), Laurent Bourgois (12), Patricia
Ciriani (13), Françoise Groshens (14), Ariane Jouannais (15), Cyrine
Busson (16), Jean-Claude Laisne (17), Alexandre Simoni (18), Michel
Ferranet (19), Maxime Ketoff (20), Olivier Chaslin (21), Patrice de Turenne
(22), Michel Dayot (23), Jean Pierre Crousse (24), Richard Henriot (25),
Nathalie du Luart (26), Laurent Tournié (27), Sandra Barclay (28), Michel
Kagan (29), Michel Bourdeau (30), Hérve Dubois (31), Miguel Macian
(32), Enrique Santillana (33), Cyrille Faivre (34), Laurent Scatola (35),
Didier Sancey (36), Dominique Neves (37), Hérve Bleton (38), David
Mangin (39), Ivan Tizianel (40).

ACKNOWLEDGEMENTS

I wish to thank Rockport Publishers and its selection committee for its interest in my work, Richard Meier and François Chaslin for their support and collaboration, Michel Desjardins, my very old friend and photographer since my first French projects, Patrick and Daniele Colombier for their unwavering support, Christian Devillers for his enthusiasm and generosity during the Evry and Lognes construction period, Alexandra Boyle for her assistance in rewriting and translating the texts, Stéphane Couturier for being such a good photographer, Marybeth Shaw for her translation of the introduction, and all those who have assisted me with the projects published in this book, mainly Vincent Sabatier, Jacky Nicolas, and Jean Pierre Crousse. But most of all I wish to thank those without whom this book would not have been possible: Jean-Marie Monthiers, whose photographs have been of great assistance to me during the past ten years and Marcela, my wife, photographer, friend, and partner who, for the past twenty years, has allowed me to focus unrestrained on the essence of design.

Dedication:

To my three women: Marcela, Laura, and Patricia